Learn Colors
With Camron and Chloe

Denver International SchoolHouse

Learn colors with Camron and Chloe

Denver International SchoolHouse

© 2020 Denver International SchoolHouse

All rights reserved. No part of this publication may be reproduced, stored in a retrieval system or transmited in any form or by any means, electronic, mechanical, photocopying, recording or otherwise without the prior permision of the publisher or in accordance with the provisions of the Copyright, Designs and Patents Act 1988 or under the terms of any licence permitting limited copying issued by the Copyright Licensing Angency.

ISBN : 978-1-7358013-1-5

Name:_____

White

Color the pictures *white*.

Name:_____

White

Color the picture that is **white** in each row.

  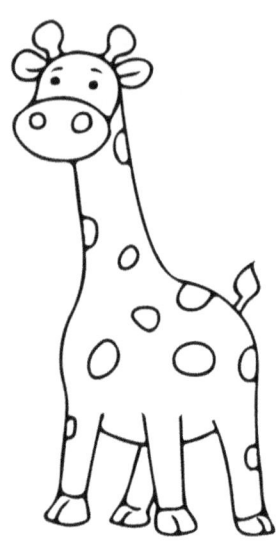

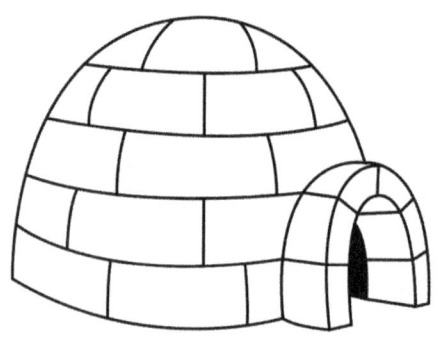  

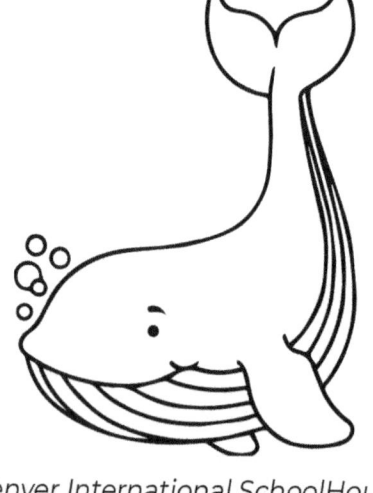  

Name:______________________

White

Draw something **white.**

Trace the word **white.**

white

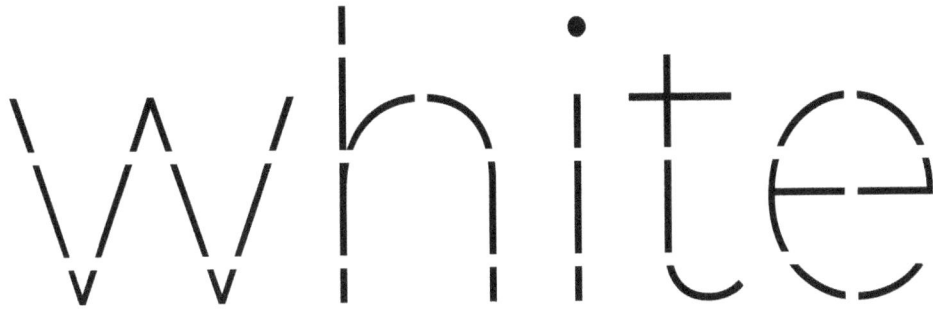

Name:_____

Color the pictures white

Denver International SchoolHouse 4

Name:_____

Trace and write the word

white | white

Color the three that could be *white*.

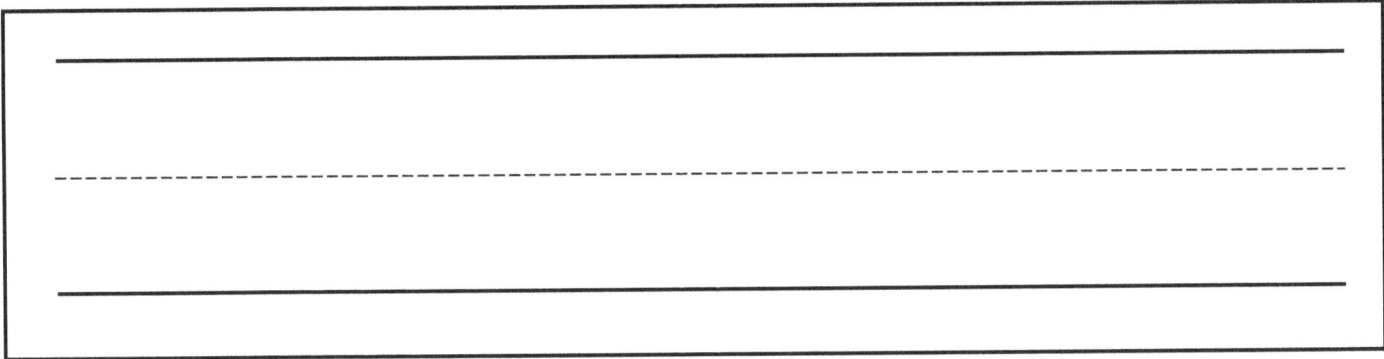

Name:_____

Color review

Color the space marked **white** with the correct crayon.

Denver International SchoolHouse

Name:_____

Red

Color the pictures **red**.

Name:_____

Red

Color the picture that is **red** in each row.

 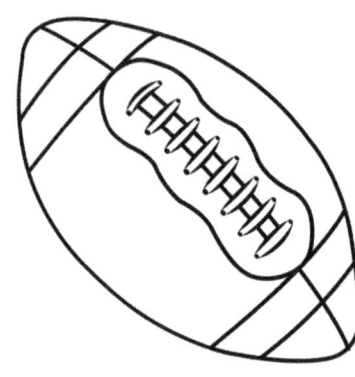 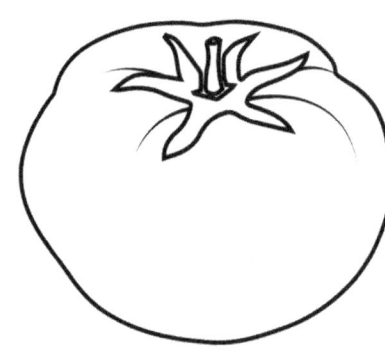

Name:____________________

Red

*Draw something **red.***

*Trace the word **red.***

red

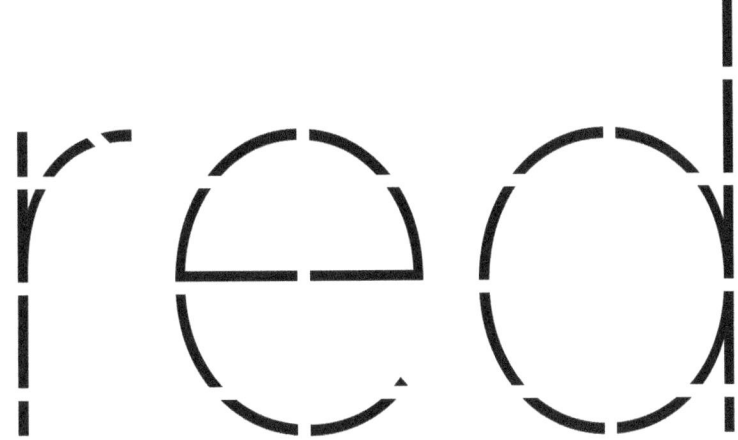

Name:_____

Color the pictures red

Denver International SchoolHouse

Name:_____

Trace and write the word

red | red

Color the three that could be *red*.

Color review

Color the space marked **red** with the correct crayon.

Name:_____

Black

Color the pictures **black**.

Name:_____

Black

Color the picture that *is* **black** in each row.

 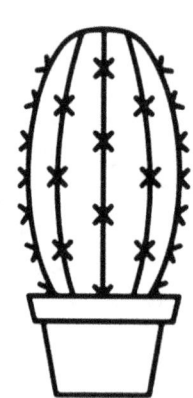 

 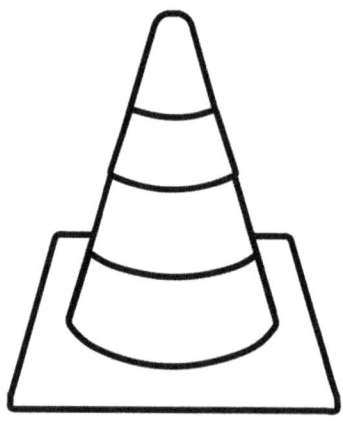 

Name:____________________

Black

Draw something **black.**

Trace the word **black.**

black

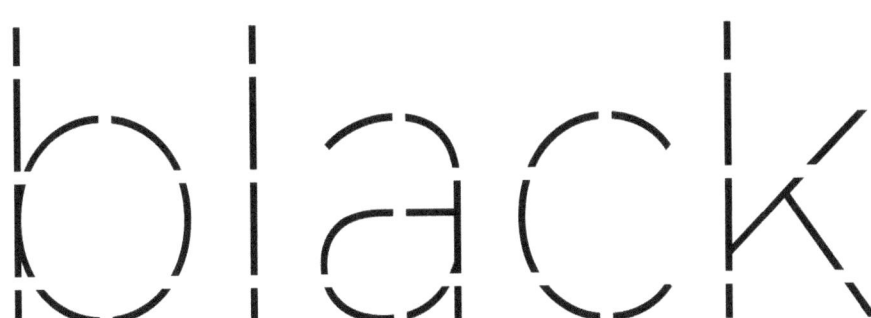

Name:_____

Color the pictures black

Denver International SchoolHouse

Name:_____

Trace and write the word

black   black

Color the three that could be **black**.

Name:_____

Color review

Color the space marked **black** with the correct crayon.

Denver International SchoolHouse

Name:_____

Orange

*Color the pictures **orange**.*

Name:_____

Orange

Color the picture that is **orange** in each row.

Denver International SchoolHouse

Name:______________________

Orange

Draw something **orange.**

Trace the word **orange.**

orange

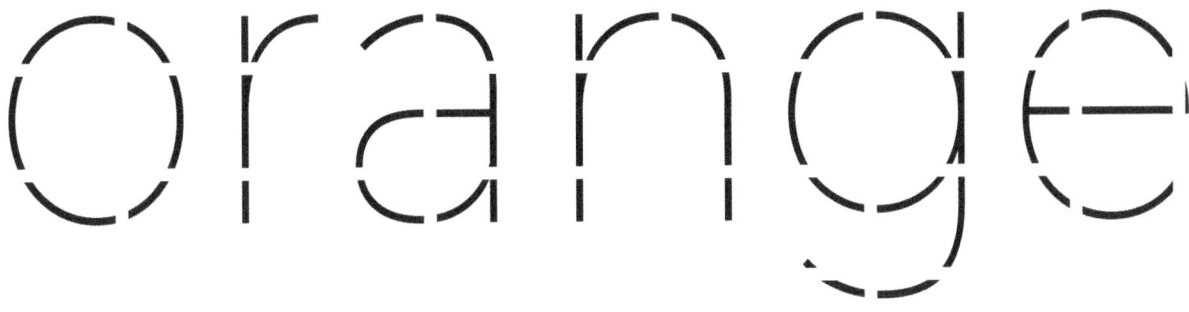

Name:_____

Color the pictures orange

Denver International SchoolHouse

Name:_____

Trace and write the word

orange | orange

Color the three that could be **orange**.

Name:_____

Color review

Color the space marked **orange** with the correct crayon.

Denver International SchoolHouse

Name:_____

Blue

Color the pictures **blue**.

Name:_____

Blue

Color the picture that is **blue** in each row.

 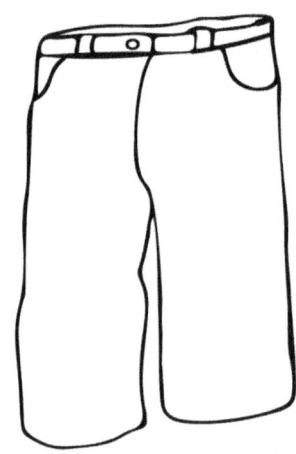 

Denver International SchoolHouse

Name:______________________

Blue

Draw something **blue.**

Trace the word **blue.**

blue

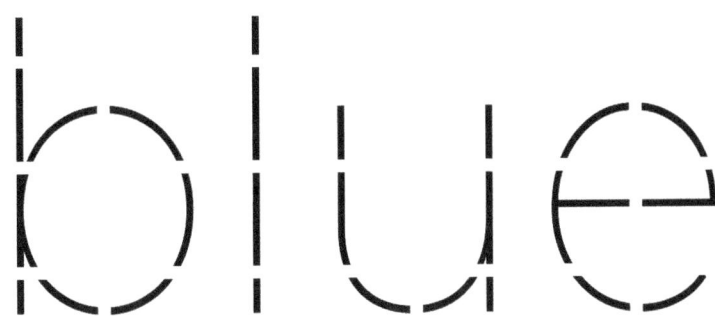

Name:_____

Color the pictures blue

Name:_____

Trace and write the word

blue | blue

Color the three that could be **blue**.

Name:_____

Color review

Color the space marked **blue** with the correct crayon.

Denver International SchoolHouse

Name:_____

Grey

*Color the pictures **grey**.*

Name:_____

Grey

Color the picture that *is* **grey** in each row.

  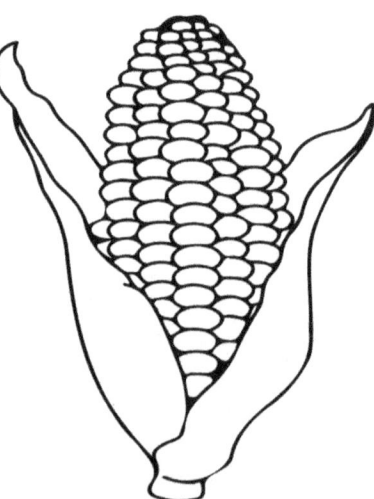

Name:____________________

Grey

*Draw something **grey.***

*Trace the word **grey.***

grey

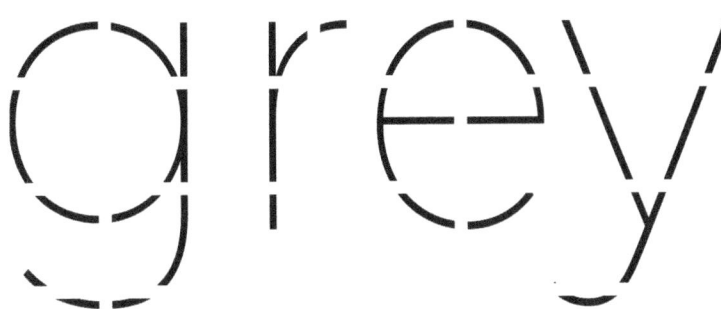

Name:_____

Color the pictures grey

Name:_____

Trace and write the word

grey   grey

Color the three that could be **grey**.

Name:_____

Color review

Color the space marked *grey* with the correct crayon.

Denver International SchoolHouse   36

Pink

Color the pictures *pink*.

Name:_____

Pink

Color the picture that is **pink** in each row.

  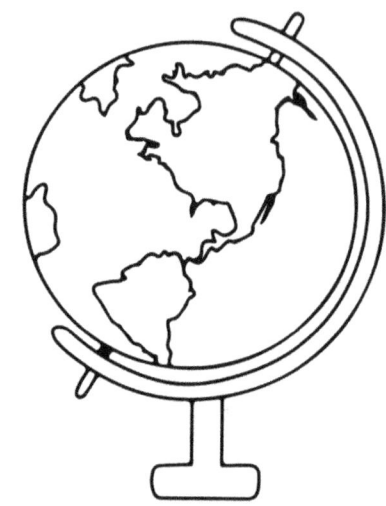

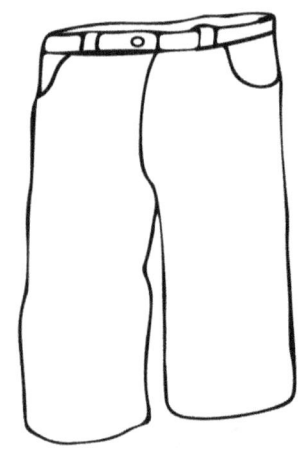  

 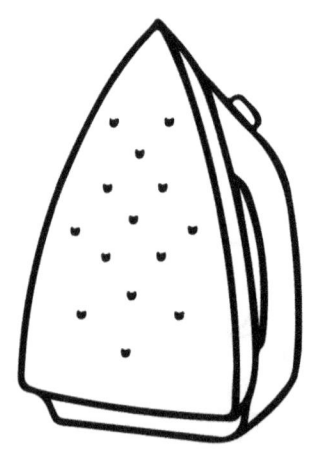 

Name:____________________

Pink

Draw something ***pink.***

Trace the word ***pink.***

pink

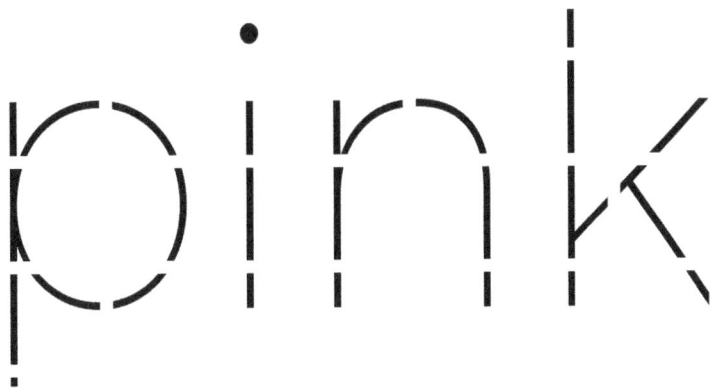

Name:_____

Color the pictures pink

Name:_____

Trace and write the word

pink   pink

Color the three that could be *pink*.

Name:_____

Color review

Color the space marked **pink** with the correct crayon.

Denver International SchoolHouse

Name:_____

Green

Color the pictures *green*.

Green

Color the picture that is **green** in each row.

 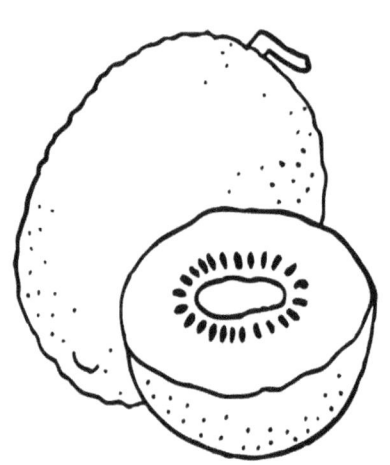 

Denver International SchoolHouse

Name:__________________

Green

*Draw something **green.***

*Trace the word **green.***

green

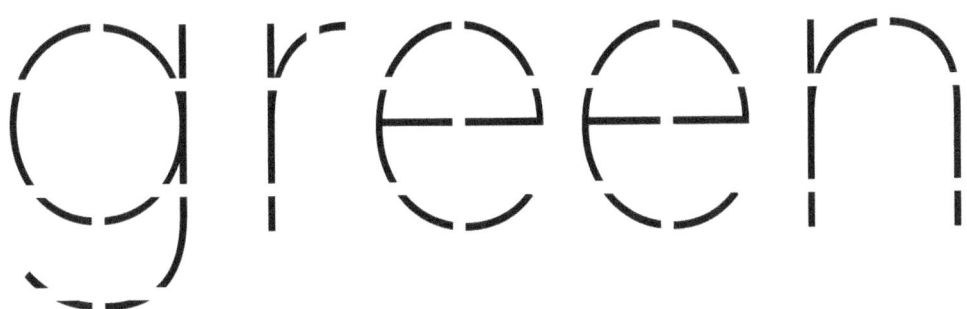

Name:_____

Color the pictures green

Name:_____

Trace and write the word

green | green

Color the three that could be **green**.

Name:_____

Color review

Color the space marked **green** with the correct crayon.

Denver International SchoolHouse   48

Name:_____

Yellow

Color the pictures *yellow*.

Name:_____

Yellow

Color the picture that is **yellow** in each row.

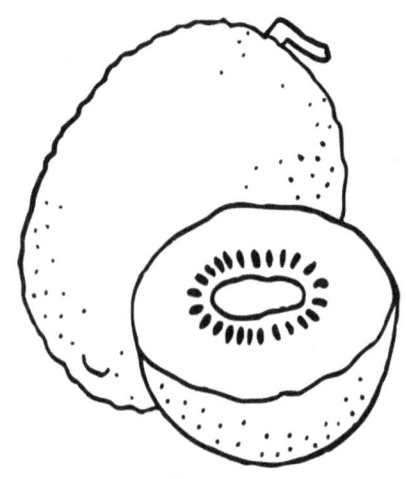  

Denver International SchoolHouse

Name:______________________

Yellow

*Draw something **yellow**.*

*Trace the word **yellow**.*

yellow

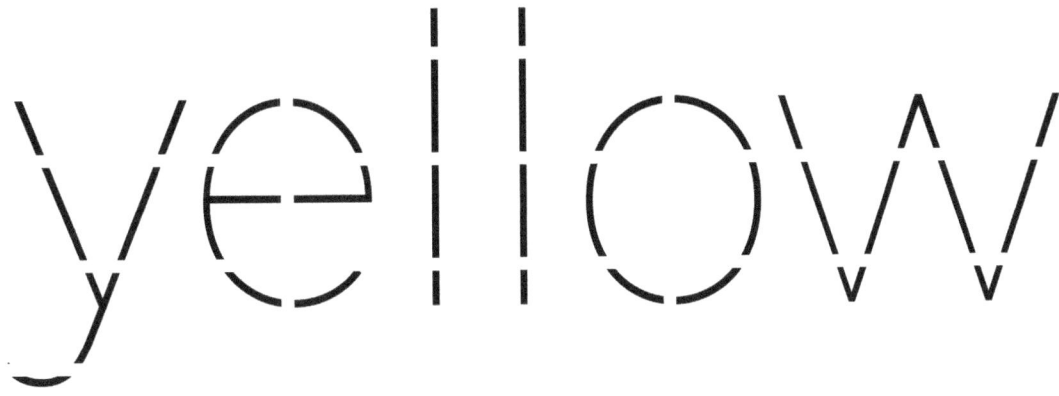

Name:_____

Color the pictures yellow

Denver International SchoolHouse

Name:_____

Trace and write the word

yellow yellow

Color the three that could be *yellow*.

Name:_____

Color review

Color the space marked *yellow* with the correct crayon.

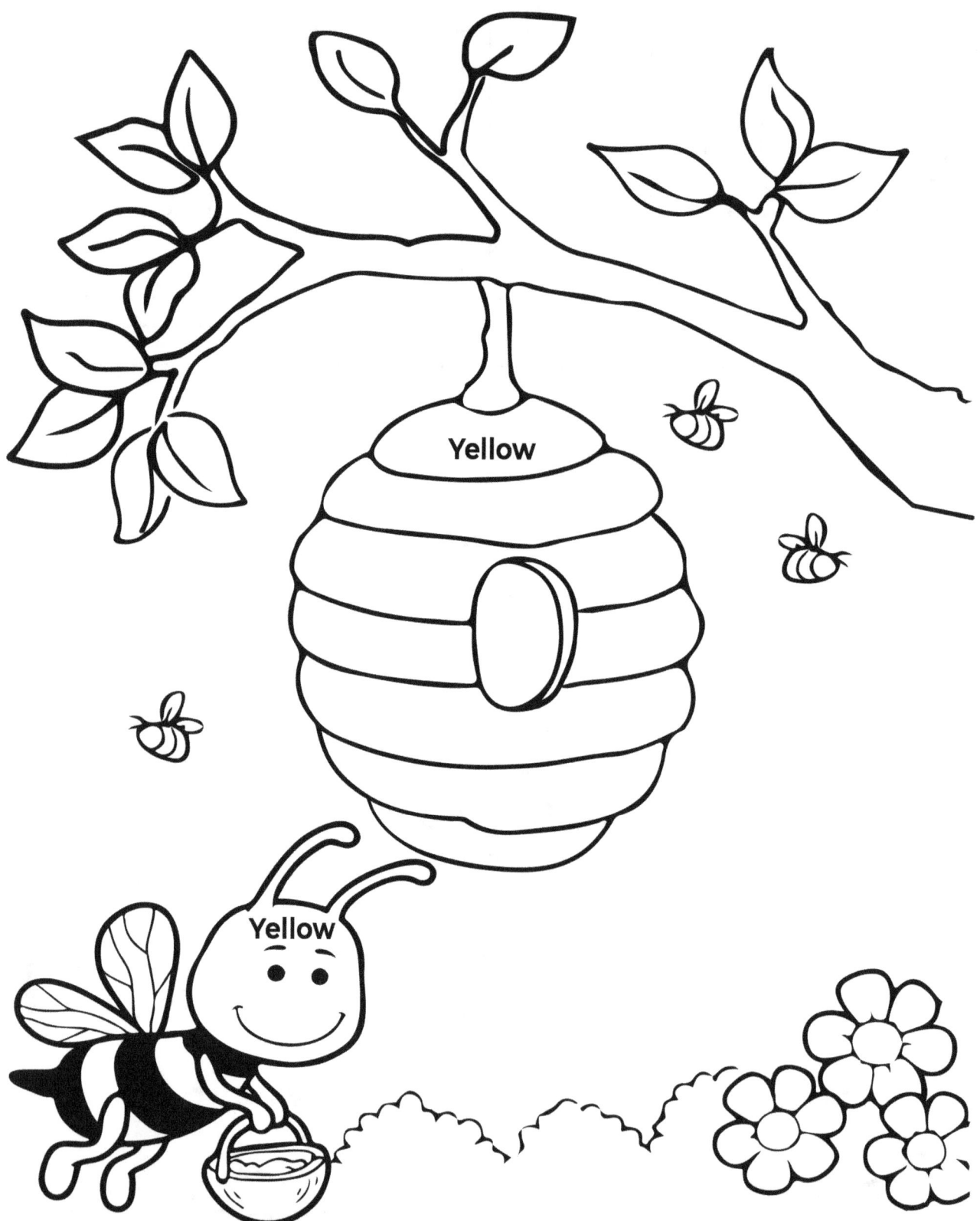

Denver International SchoolHouse

Name:_____

Purple

*Color the pictures **purple**.*

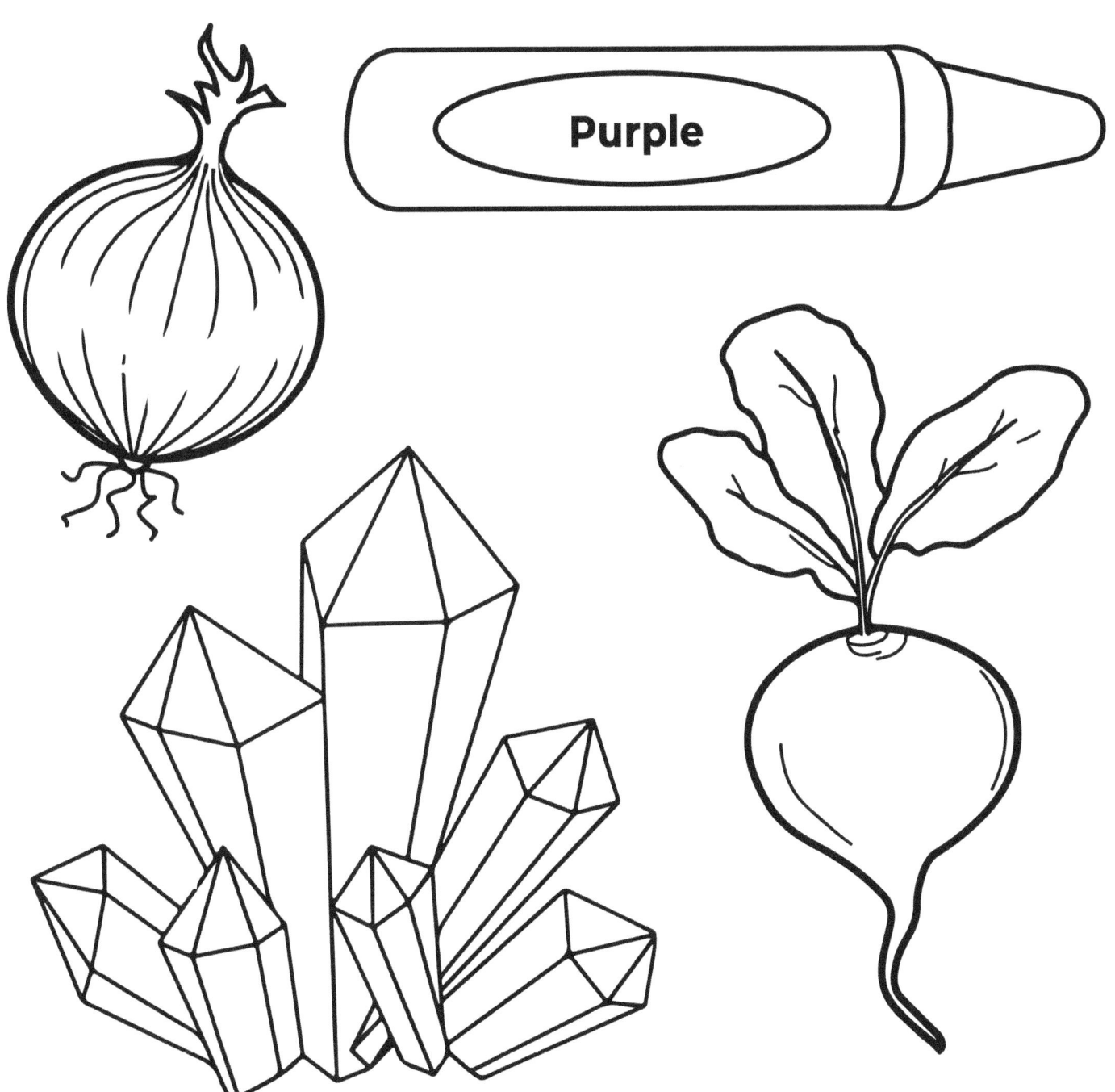

Name:_____

Purple

Color the picture that is **purple** in each row.

Denver International SchoolHouse

Name:________________

Purple

Draw something **purple.**

Trace the word **purple.**

purple

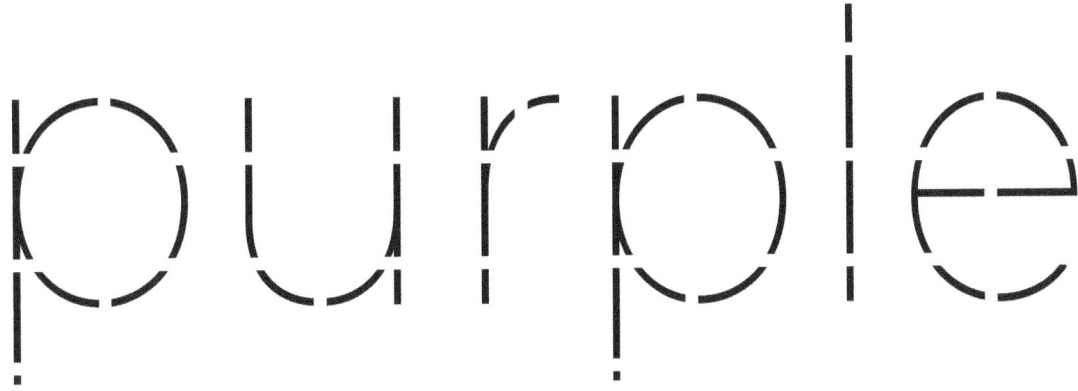

Name:_____

Color the pictures purple

Denver International SchoolHouse

Name:_____

Trace and write the word

purple   purple

Color the three that could be *purple*.

Name:_____

Color review

Color the space marked *purple* with the correct crayon.

Denver International SchoolHouse

Name:_____

Color review

Color the marked space with the correct crayon.

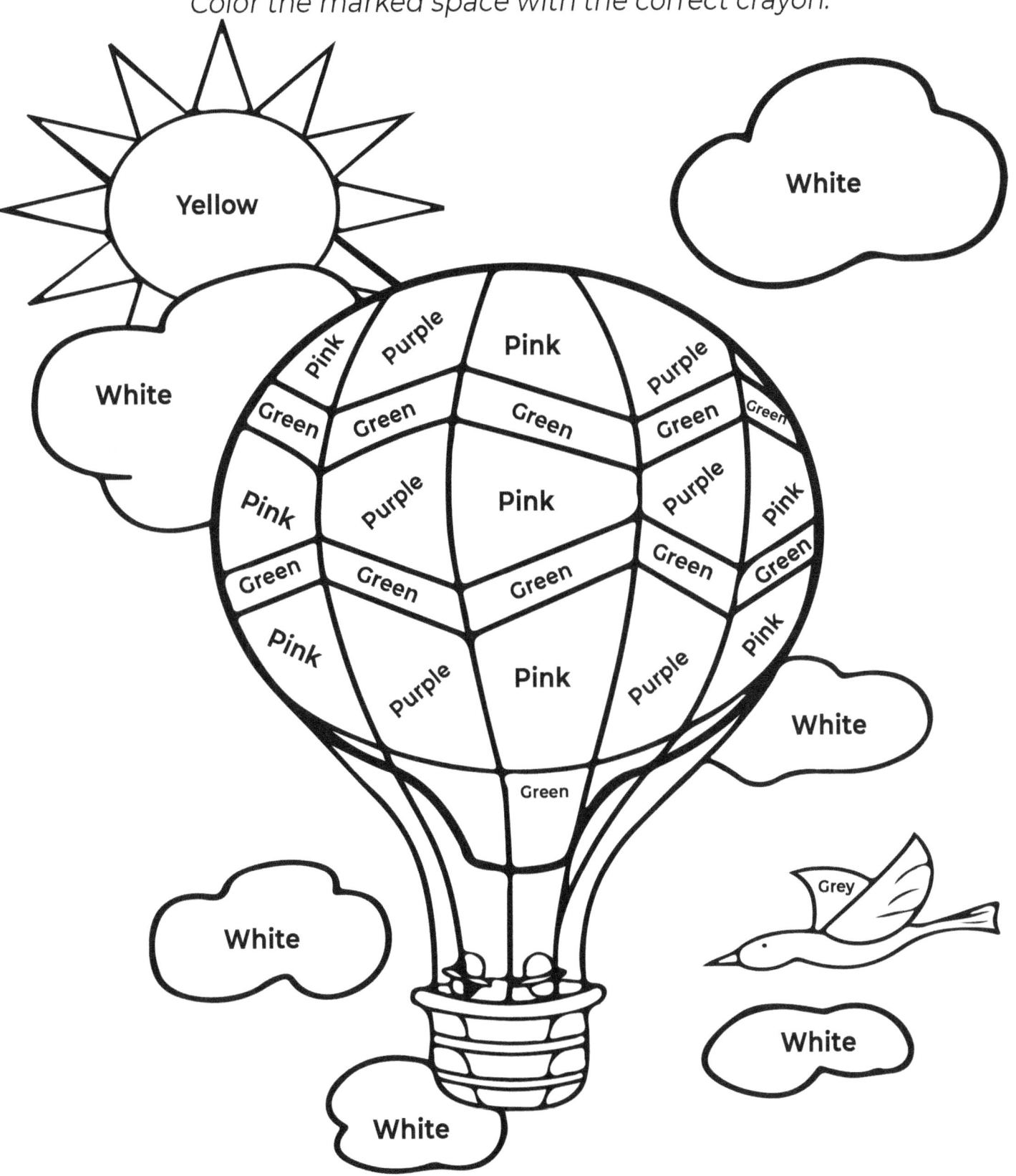

Name:_____

Color review

Color the marked space with the correct crayon.

1- White
2- Red
3- Black
4- Orange
5- Blue
6- Grey
7- Pink
8- Green
9- Yellow
10- Purple

Name:_____

Color review

Color and draw a line so that each image matches with the crayon of the same color.

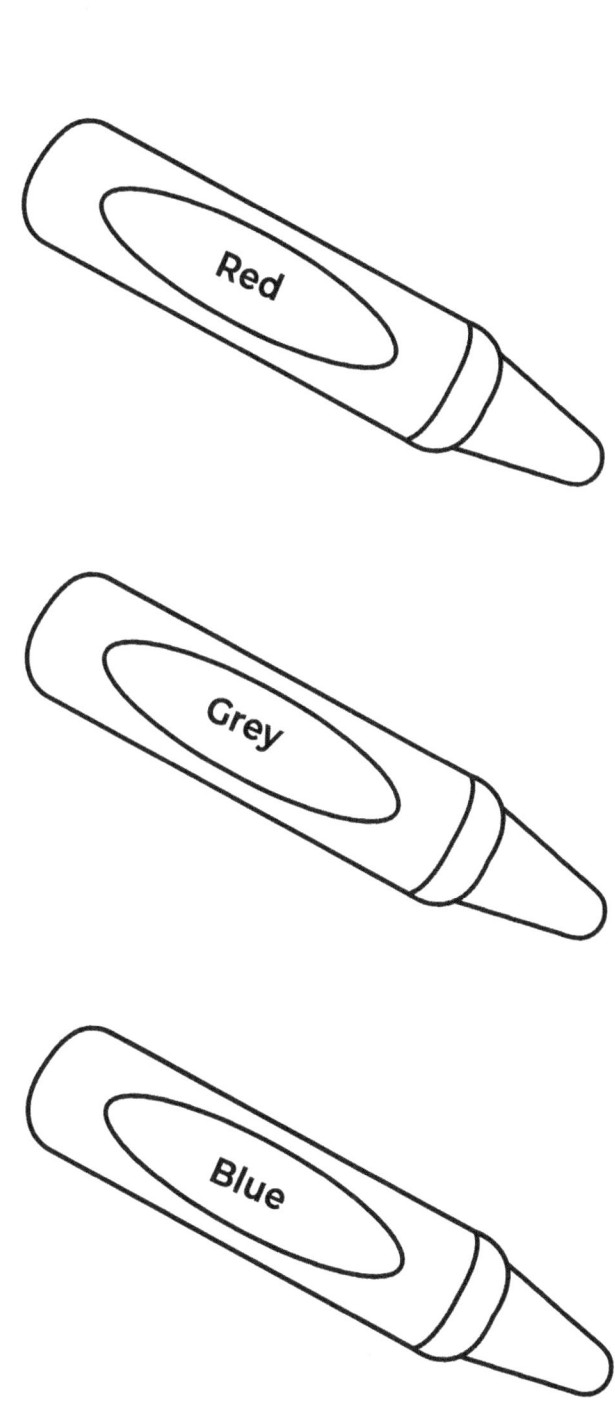

Name:_____

Color review

Color inside the words with the correct crayon.

Yellow

Blue

Red

Black

Denver International SchoolHouse

ns:_____

Color review

Color the marked space with the correct crayon.

Name:_____

Color review

Color the marked space with the correct crayon.

1- Pink
2- Green
3- Yellow
4- Purple
5- Blue
6- Grey
7- White
8- Red
9- Black
10- Orange

Denver International SchoolHouse

Name:_____

Color review

Color and draw a line so that each image matches
with the crayon of the same color.

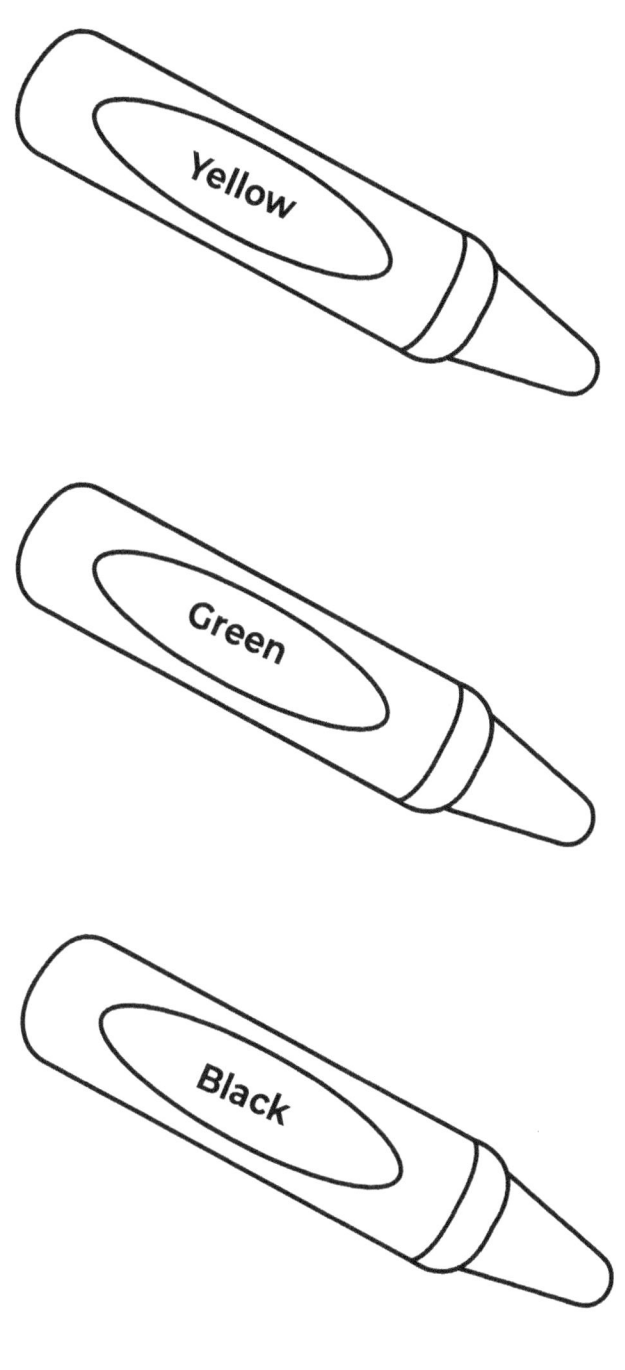

Name:_____

Color review

Color inside the words with the correct crayon.

Orange
Green
Pink
White

Name:_____

Color review

Color the marked space with the correct crayon.

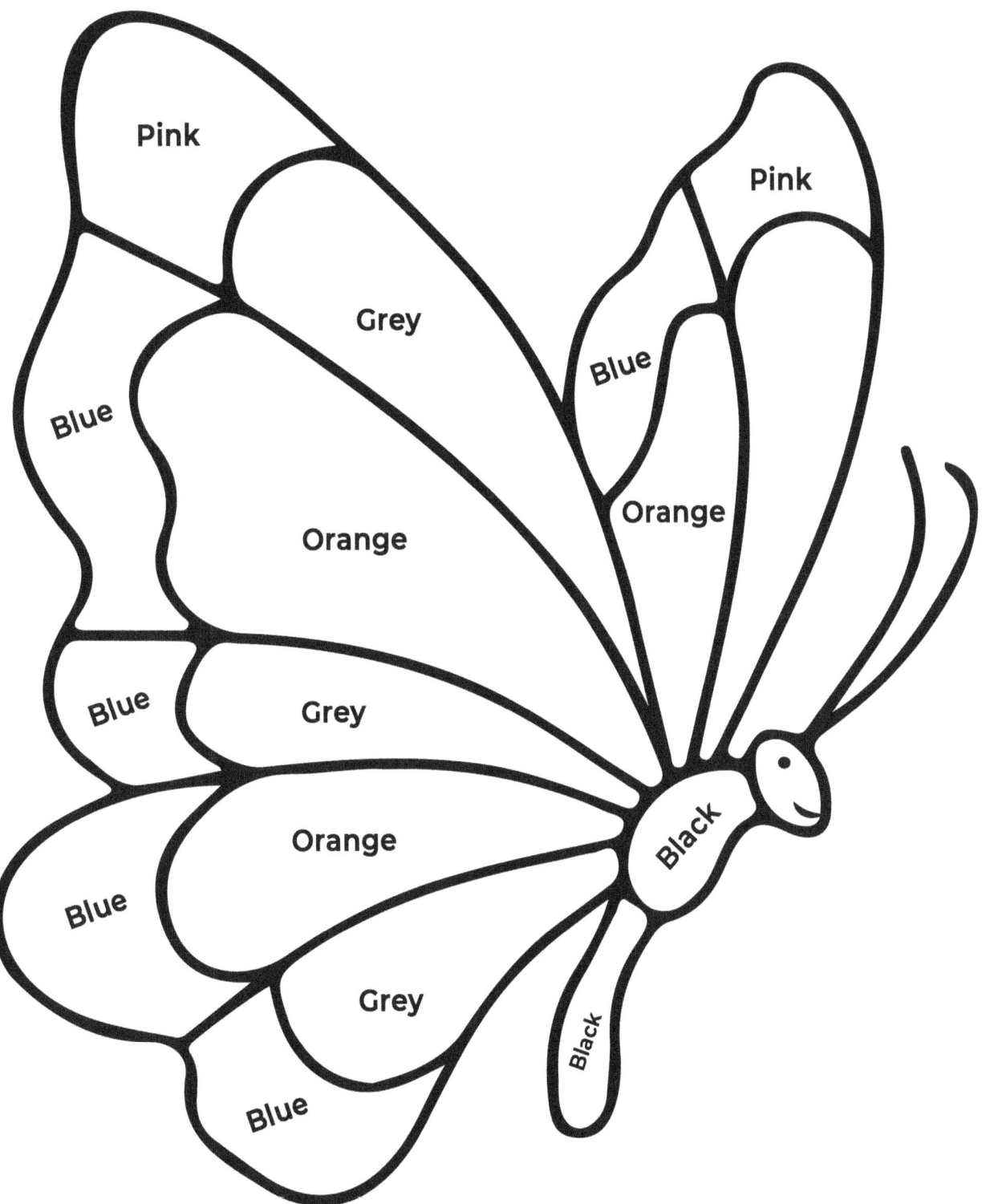

69   Denver International SchoolHouse

Name:_____

Color review

Color the marked space with the correct crayon.

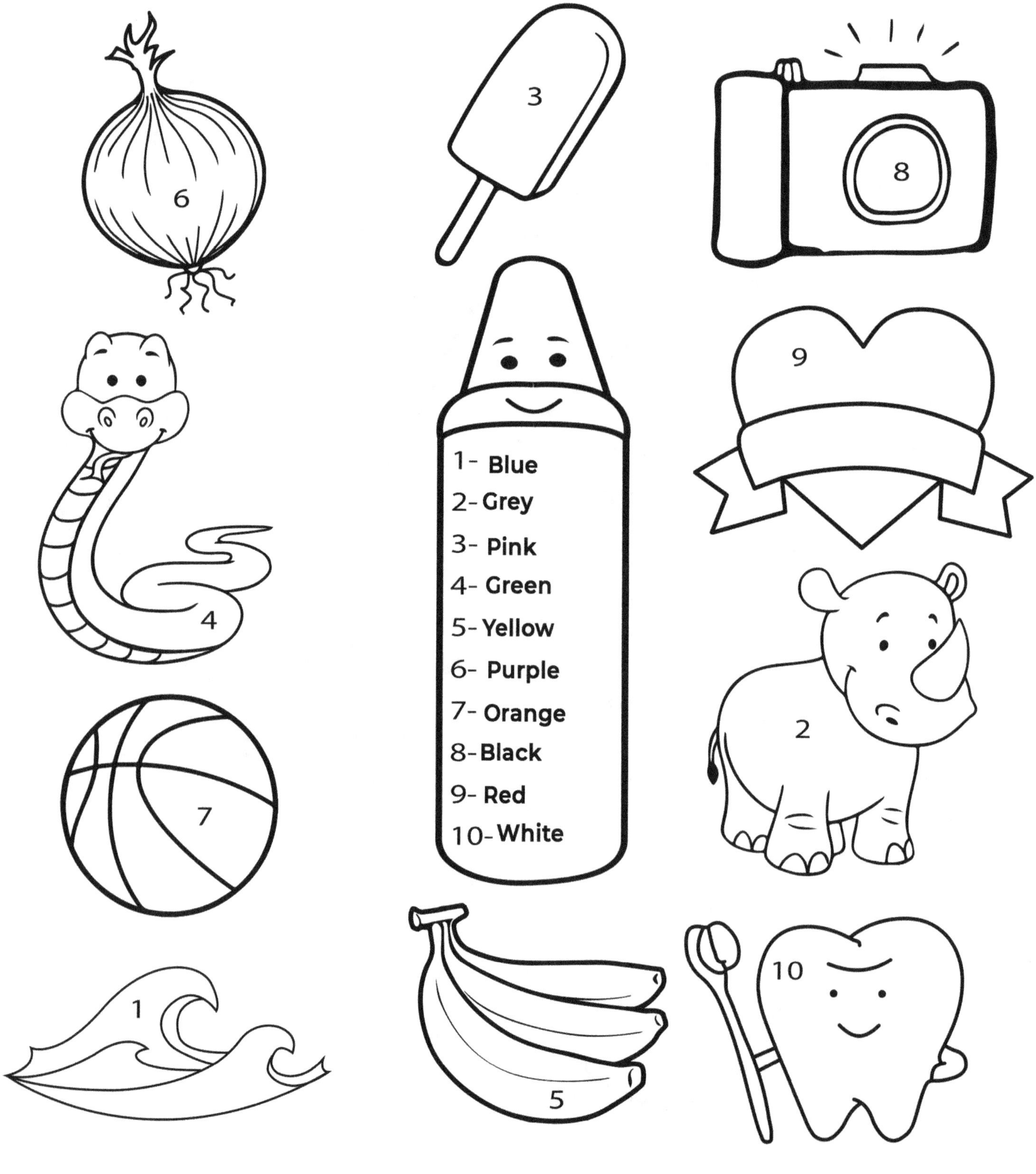

1- Blue
2- Grey
3- Pink
4- Green
5- Yellow
6- Purple
7- Orange
8- Black
9- Red
10- White

Name:_____

Color review

Color and draw a line so that each image matches with the crayon of the same color.

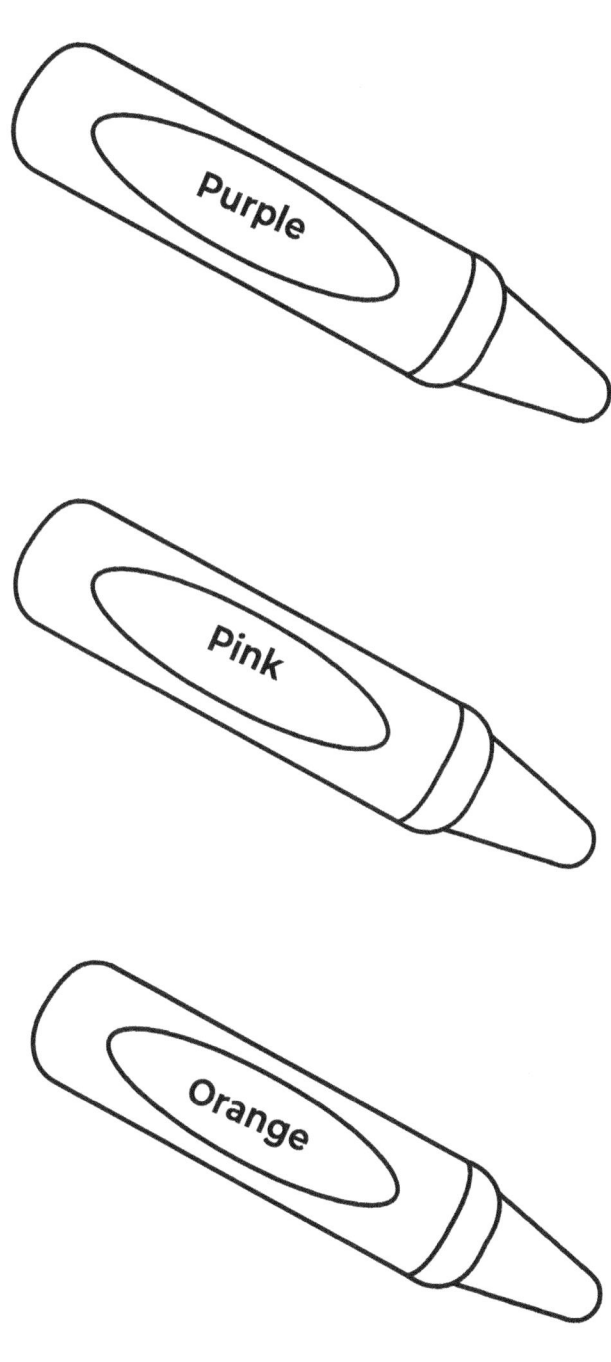

71 Denver International SchoolHouse

Name:_____

Color review

Color inside the words with the correct crayon.

Purple
Red
Grey
Green

Denver International SchoolHouse

Name:_____

Color review

Color the marked space with the correct crayon.

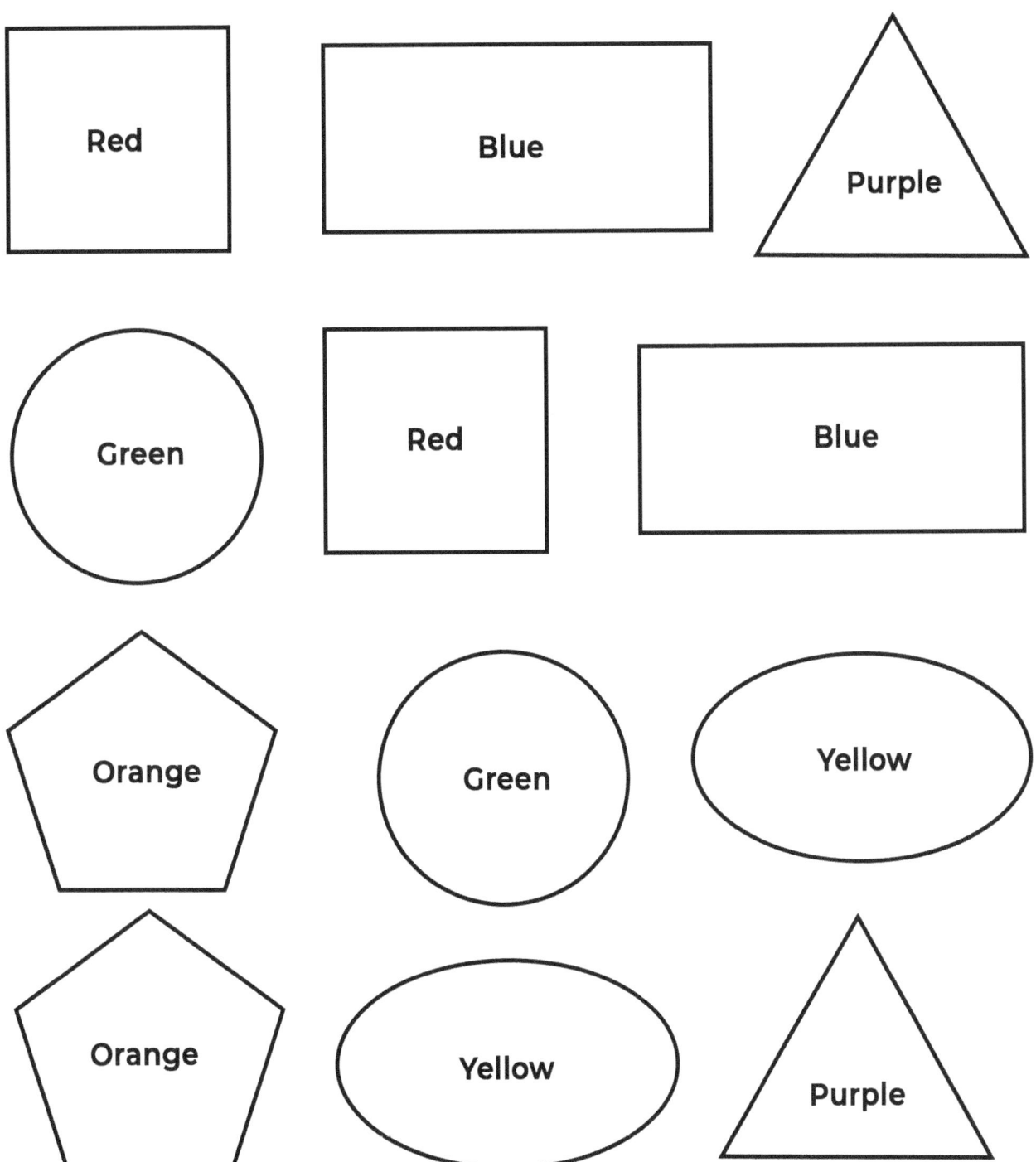

73   Denver International SchoolHouse

Name:_____

Color review

Color the marked space with the correct crayon.

1- Orange
2- Green
3- White
4- Red
5- Blue
6- Grey
7- Yellow
8- Purple
9- Black
10- Pink

Denver International SchoolHouse

Color review

Name:_____

Color and draw a line so that each image matches with the crayon of the same color.

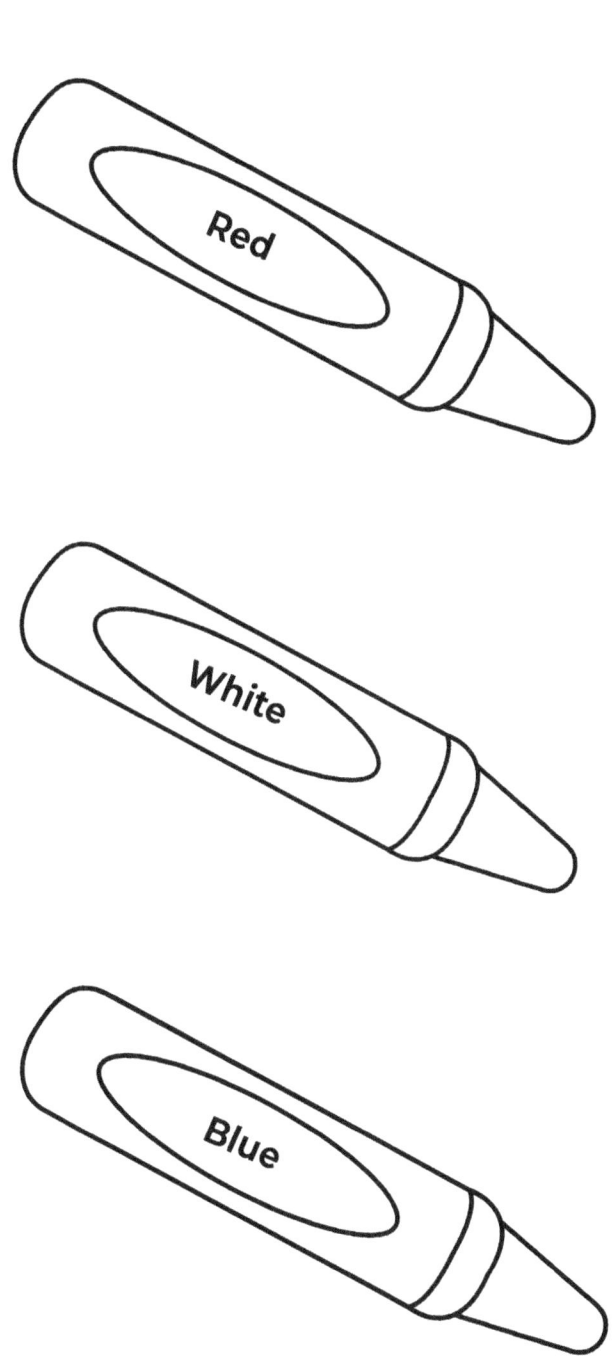
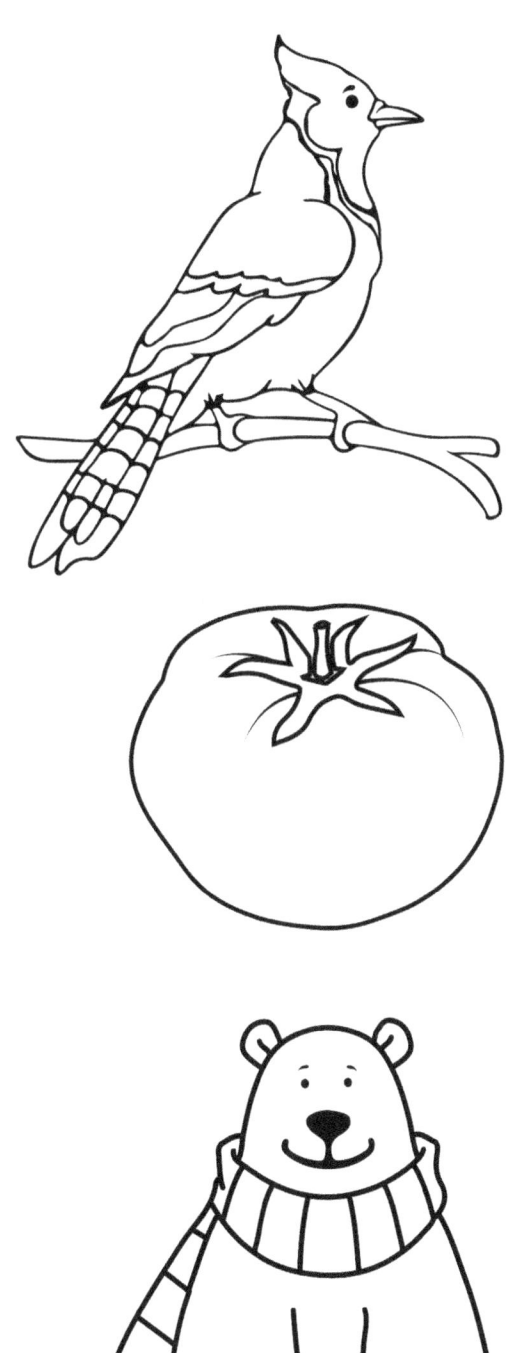

Name:_____

Color review

Observe the sequence of each row and color the one that follows according to the sequence.

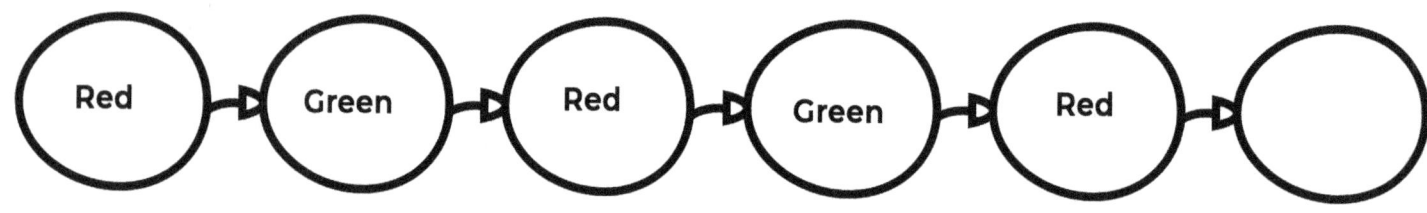

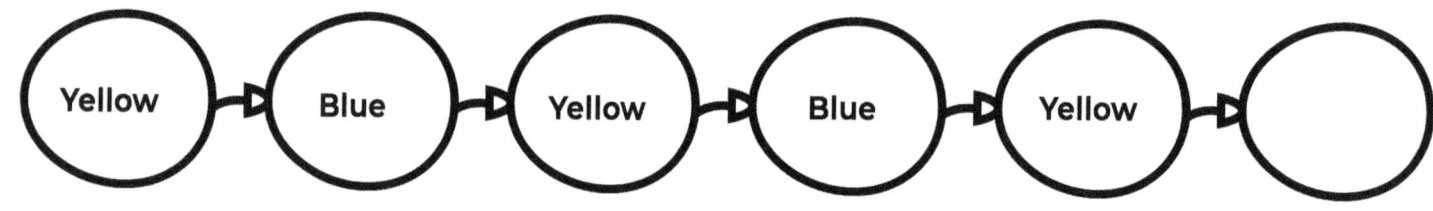

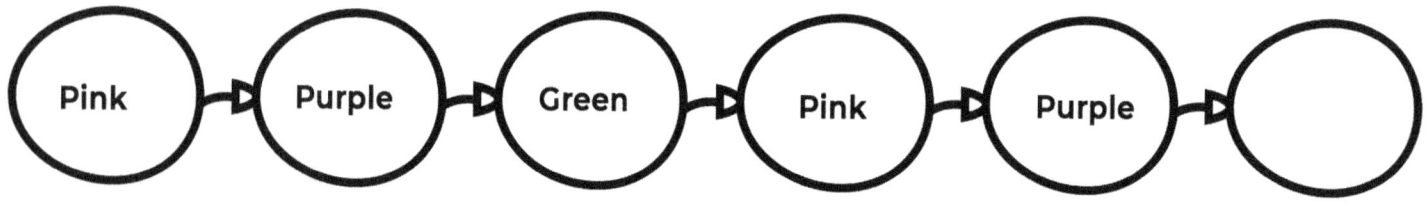

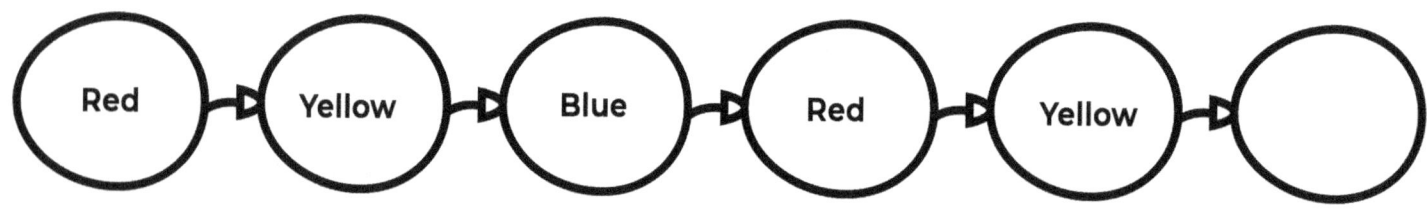

Name:_____

Color review

Color the marked letter with the correct crayon.

A = White
B = Red
C = Black
D = Orange
E = Blue

77 Denver International SchoolHouse

Name:______________________

Color review

Color the marked space with the correct crayon.

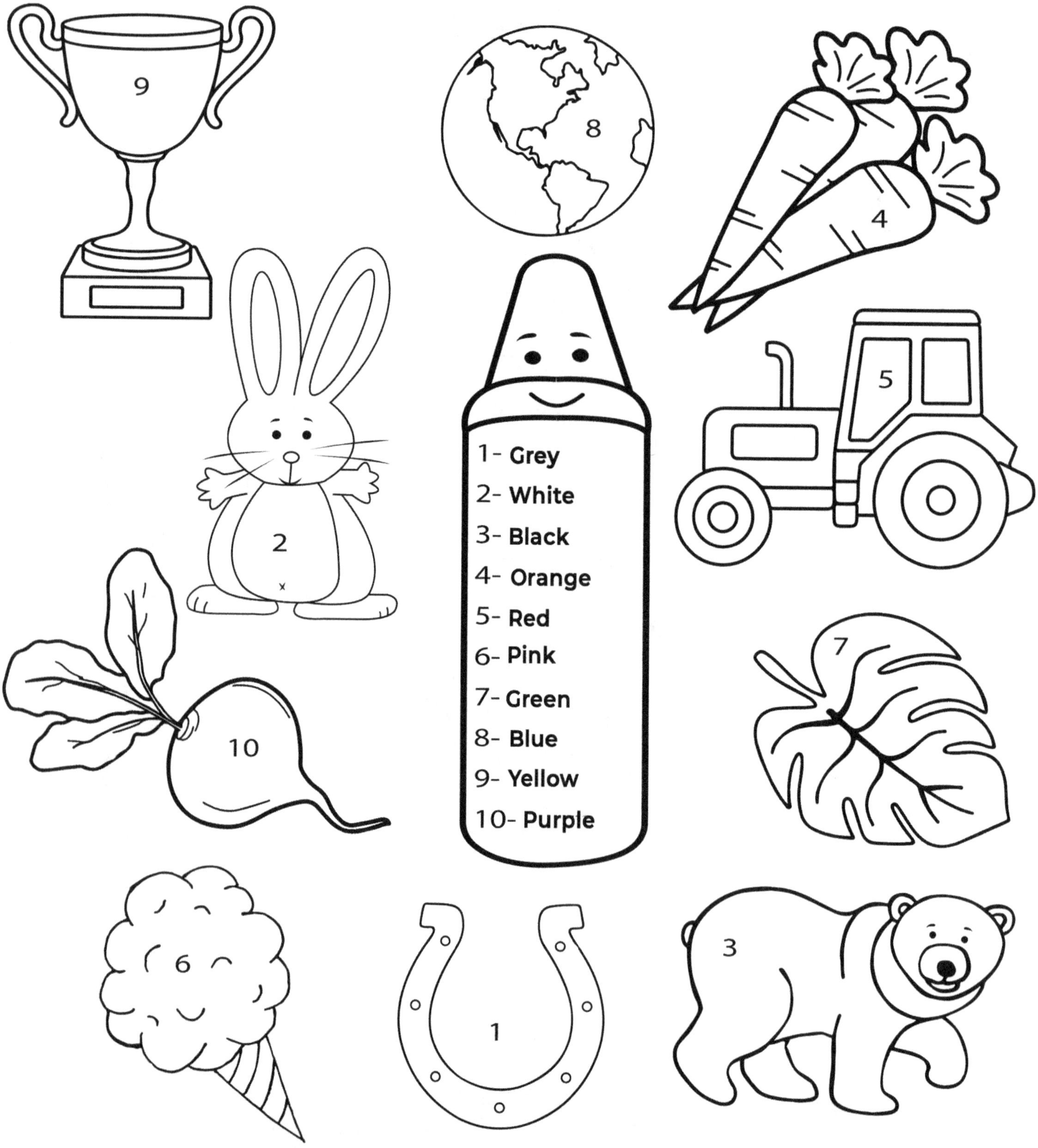
9
8
4
5
2
1- Grey
2- White
3- Black
4- Orange
5- Red
6- Pink
7- Green
8- Blue
9- Yellow
10- Purple
10
7
6
1
3

Name:_____

Color review

Color and draw a line so that each image matches with the crayon of the same color.

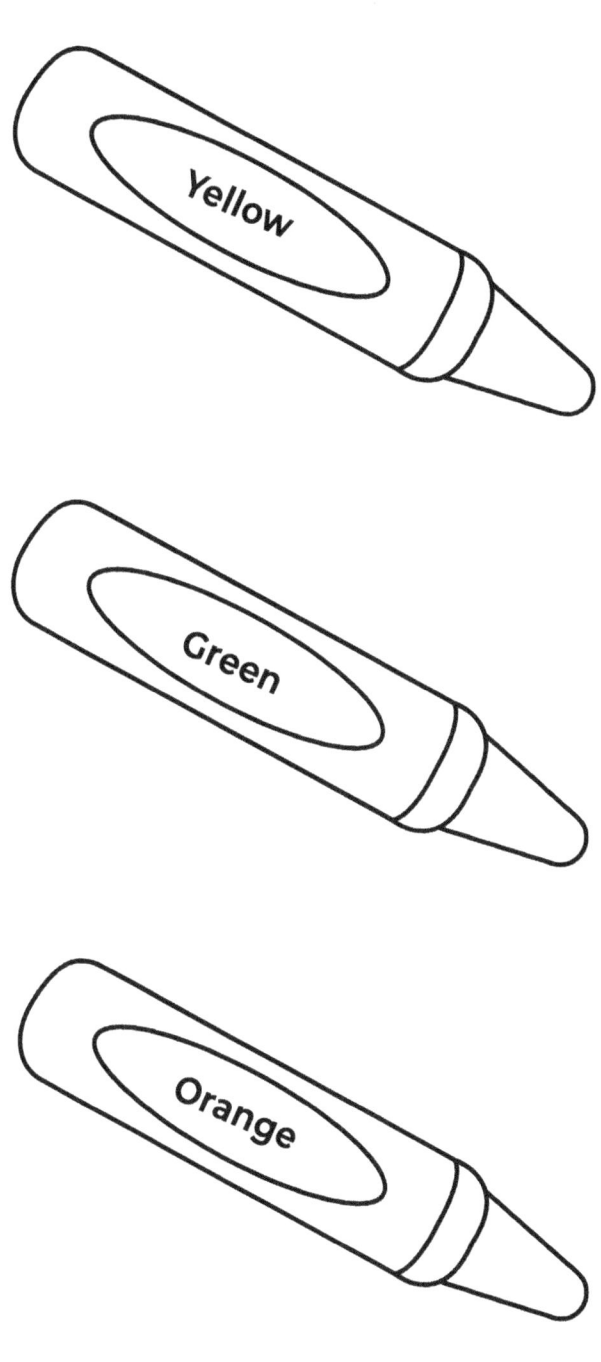
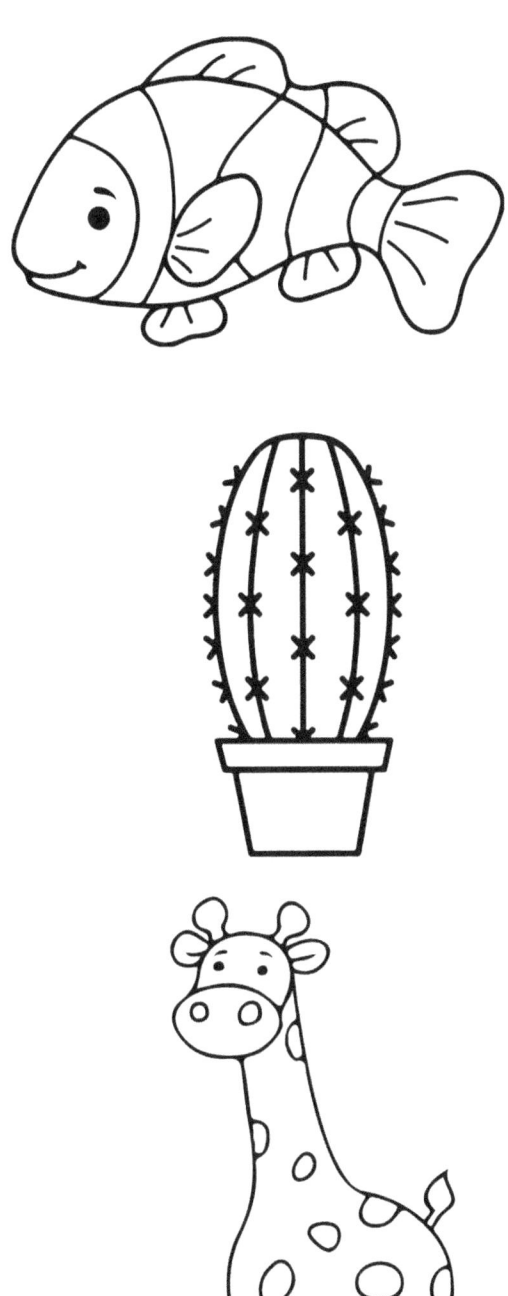

79   Denver International SchoolHouse

Color review

Color the marked letter with the correct crayon.

A = White
B = Red
C = Green
D = Yellow
E = Blue

Denver International SchoolHouse

Contact Us:

Web: www.dispreschool.com

Phone: (303) 928-7535

Facebook: @dispreschool

Twitter: @DISPreschool

Address: 6295 S Main St B113, Aurora, CO 80016

www.ingramcontent.com/pod-product-compliance
Lightning Source LLC
Chambersburg PA
CBHW081420080526
44589CB00016B/2610